8658

Gift 2001

BLOOMFIELD PUBLIC LIBRARY
New Bloomfield, PA 17068

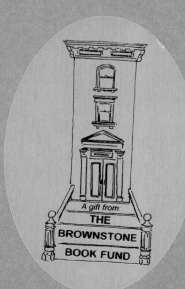

A gift from
THE
BROWNSTONE
BOOK FUND

Cherry Pies and Lullabies

LYNN REISER

Cherry Pies and Lullabies

Greenwillow Books　New York

BLOOMFIELD PUBLIC LIBRARY
New Bloomfield, PA 17068

8658

**With thanks to John Forster for his help
in arranging the lullaby**

The designs of all the quilts are variations
of the American quilt pattern "Cherry Basket."

Watercolor paints and a black pen were used for the full-color art.
The text type is Kuenstler 480.
Copyright © 1998 by Lynn Whisnant Reiser
All rights reserved. No part of this book may be reproduced or utilized in any form
or by any means, electronic or mechanical, including photocopying, recording, or by any
information storage and retrieval system, without permission in writing from the Publisher,
Greenwillow Books, a division of William Morrow & Company, Inc.,
1350 Avenue of the Americas, New York, NY 10019.
http://www.williammorrow.com
Printed in Singapore by Tien Wah Press
First Edition 10 9 8 7 6 5 4 3 2

Library of Congress Cataloging-in-Publication Data
Reiser, Lynn.
Cherry pies and lullabies / by Lynn Reiser.
p.   cm.
Summary: Four generations of mothers and daughters express
their love through family traditions that are the same but different.
ISBN 0-688-13391-6 (trade).   ISBN 0-688-13392-4 (lib. bdg.)
[1. Mothers and daughters—Fiction.   2. Grandmothers—Fiction.]
I. Title.   PZ7.R27745Ce   1998   [E]—dc20
95-2259   CIP   AC

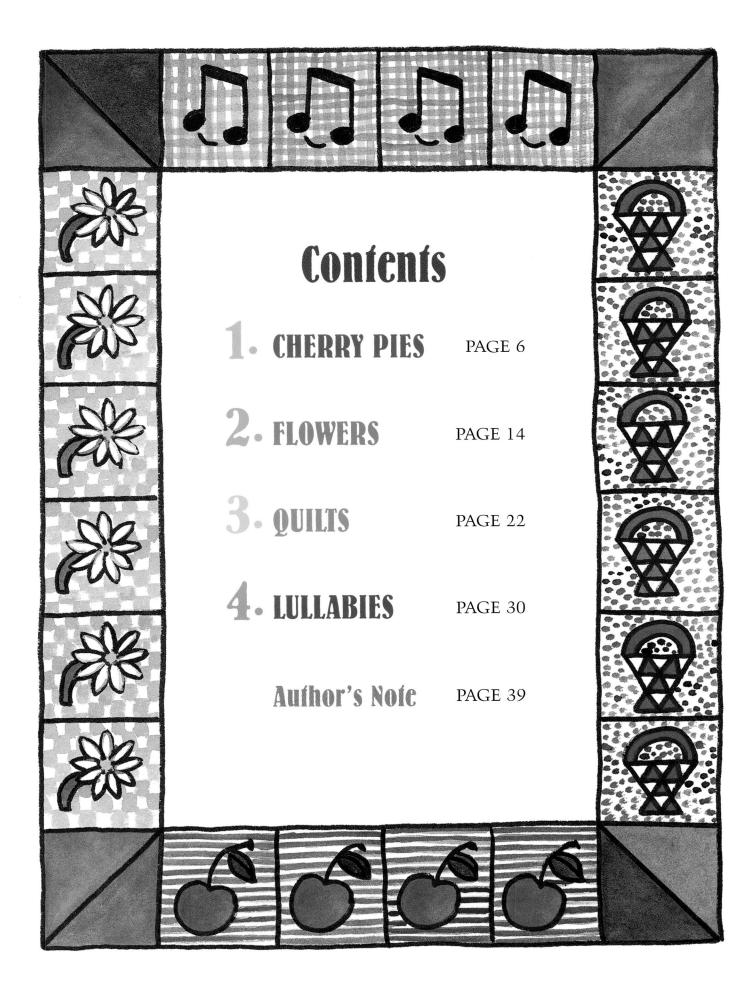

Contents

.1.
Cherry Pies

My great-grandmother
baked a cherry pie
for my grandmother;

my grandmother
baked a cherry pie
for my mother;

my mother
baked a cherry pie
for me;

and I
baked a cherry pie
for my bear.

Every time
it was the same,
but different.

·2·
Flowers

My great-grandmother
made a crown of flowers
for my grandmother;

my grandmother
made a crown of flowers
for my mother;

my mother made
a crown of flowers
for me;

and I made
a crown of flowers
for my bear.

Every time
it was the same,
but different.

.3.
Quilts

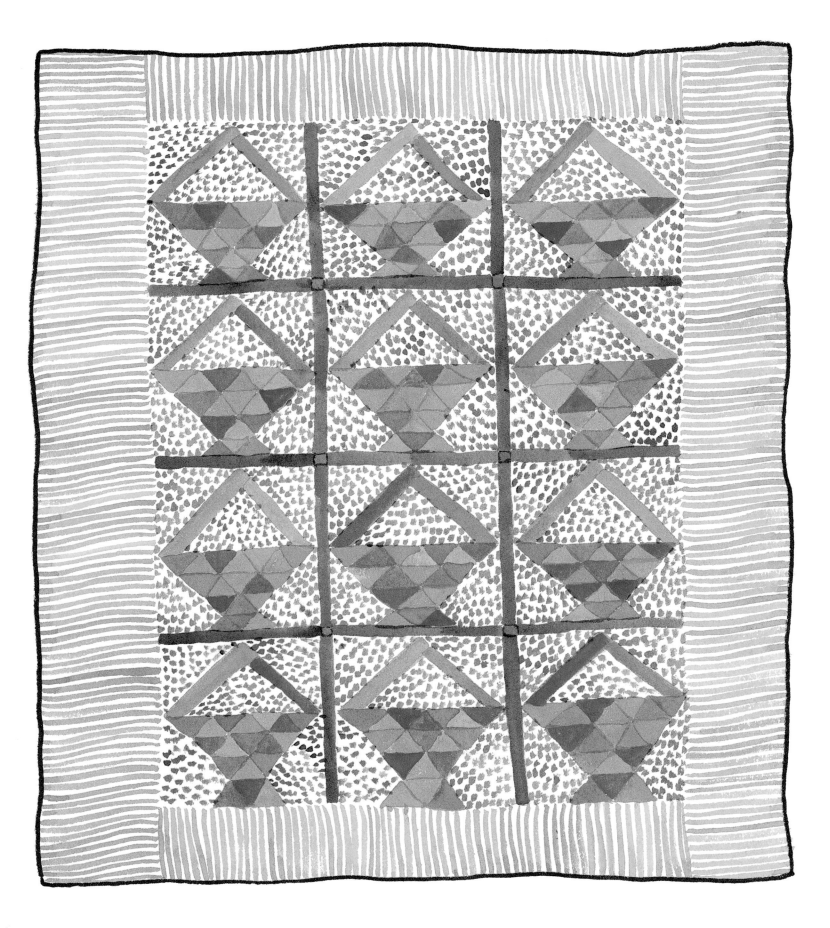

23

My great-grandmother
gave a quilt
to my grandmother;

my grandmother
gave a quilt
to my mother;

BLOOMFIELD PUBLIC LIBRARY
New Bloomfield, PA 17068

8658

my mother
gave a quilt
to me;

and
I gave a quilt
to my bear.

Every time
it was the same,
but different.

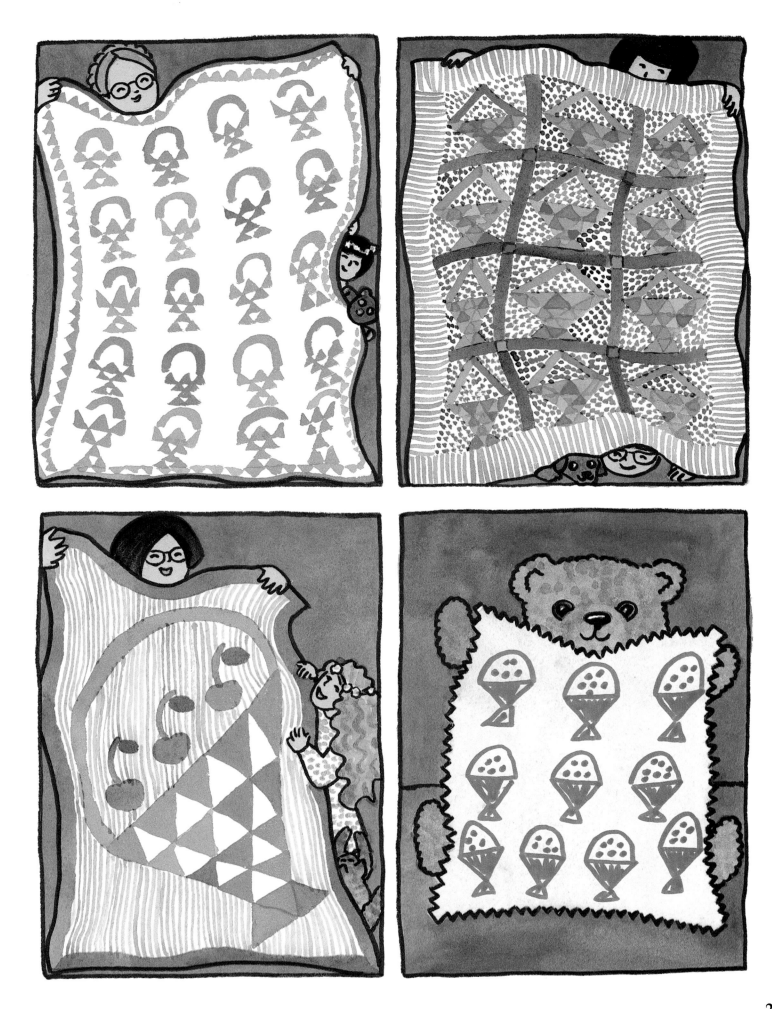

.4.
Lullabies

My great-grandmother
sang a lullaby
to my grandmother;

my grandmother
sang a lullaby
to my mother;

my mother
sang a lullaby
to me;

I sang
a lullaby
to my bear.

And every time
it was the same.

LULLABY

LYNN REISER

BRAHMS' "LULLABY"

Lul – la- by and good–night. Pie is sweet, stars are

bright.__ Close your eyes__ un – til day.__ In your

dreams__ laugh and play. Crowned with flow – ers you

sleep,__ wrapped in love soft and deep.__ Close your

eyes__ now and stay__ wrapped in love un - til day.

GREAT–GRANDMOTHER'S HOUSE

GRANDMOTHER'S HOUSE

MOTHER'S HOUSE

AUTHOR'S NOTE

My grandmother grew up on a farm. My mother grew up in a small town. I grew up in a suburb. My niece, Alex, is growing up in a city. In four generations life has changed for the women in my family. What was a way of life for my grandmother, and nostalgia for my mother, has become tradition for me and play for Alex. This book began with a wish to share with Alex how life once was, how much it has changed, and also to affirm how much has stayed the same.

Technology and social upheaval have had an impact in every country. Alex's mother, Branka, was born far away. As a young girl she traveled across oceans and continents to a new home, learned a new language and new customs. Her life now is different from her grandmother's and her mother's, but it is also the same. She finds new ways to continue old customs.

So this book is for Alex—and for Branka, and for mothers and daughters everywhere. In this book I share with them traditions in my family. For each generation of parents and children daily life is different, but family traditions of loving—like lullabies—are always the same.

For Fronie Moma,

Lilibel, Susan—and Alex